Gospel and Sacrament

Reclaiming a Holistic Evangelical Spirituality

Philip Seddon

Department of Theology, University of Birmingham

GROVE BOOKS LIMITED
RIDLEY HALL RD CAMBRIDGE CB3 9HU

Contents

Acknowledgments

I am grateful to the Grove Spirituality Group and Mark Mills-Powell for their encouragement to present earlier drafts of this document to two different groups. I also thank Christopher Cocksworth for his encouragement, and Allan Anderson, Liz Hoare, David Runcorn, Roly Riem, Debbie Seddon, Pete Wilcox and Tim Yates for specific advice and comments. But my major gratitude goes to (Bishop) Tom Wright for his generous and detailed critical comments earlier on, and my son Nicholas for his extremely helpful and incisive last-minute critique.

Beyond that, I wish to thank all our Catholic and Orthodox friends, too numerous to name, who have shaped our lives so deeply through discussion and worship. Even with all its faults, this booklet owes more to them than they know.

First Impression May 2004
ISSN 0262-799X
ISBN 1 85174 563 7

Overture: A Lost Cause?

This essay offers an Evangelical[1] Anglican re-appraisal of the sacrament of Holy Communion, in the hope of reclaiming lost territory.

I will firstly clear the ground briefly, by exposing some of the unconscious suspicions and trends which have nourished ambivalence and embarrassment. I will argue that the sacramental practice of Conservative and Charismatic Evangelicalism alike have become increasingly flawed by their shared dependence on the long Evangelical suspicion of 'sacramentalism' in any form, to the point where the sacrament has almost been evacuated of any meaning. I will then reflect on a crucial but sidelined foundation of Christian doctrine, and finally offer biblical and theological reasons as to why Anglican Evangelicals should honour the sacrament more generously than they do.

My focus on practice as much as on theology is deliberate, and based on the cultural observation that more can often be learnt about subliminal (and often denied) attitudes from what actually goes on than by any amount of scratching through politically correct documents. The impressionistic, rather than exclusively text-based, approach is therefore not accidental, and is, in addition, based on 40 years' experience of and reflection on a wide range of Evangelical Anglican churches.

Evangelicanism has become more—not less—embarrassed about the sacraments than before

It is worth making two initial state-of-play points. The first is an issue of *cultural history*, illustrated by a brief 1958 paper on the Lord's Supper by Alan Stibbs.[2] Stibbs is traditionally Evangelical in his biblical exposition, and courteous, on the whole, in disagreement, but noticeably refers to 'the sacrament,' 'the sacramental action' or 'the sacramental movement' some 14 times in just over six pages of text. This suggests that, despite over 40 years of charismatic and ecumenical movements, Evangelicalism has become more—not less—embarrassed about the sacraments than before. Today, many Evangelicals never use the word.

The second point is that of *modulation* and *nuance* in theology. Despite St Paul's formidable ability in his letters to argue with a whole range of rhetorical and theological subtlety, we seem to inhabit a church which is often tragically unable to live with paradox or truths held in tension at a deep level.[3] The purpose of this essay is to gather up many of the fragments that remain and to re-build a fragmented vision. This task requires a sense of cultural as well as of theological history, and a readiness to make judgements on fine points of distinction. The issue is the integrity of the gospel.

> *The purpose of this essay is to rebuild a fragmented vision*

I therefore now enumerate ten factors which hinder serious Evangelical thinking about the sacrament of Holy Communion.

First Movement: Mere Sacraments 2

1. **Anti-catholic motivation** remains high in Evangelical circles, whether in the outspoken form of Ian Paisley, or as a rippling unconscious undercurrent. Aspects of this war are embedded in our genetic history, producing a whole range of routinely paraded Aunt Sallies (whether of any form of ritual or symbolism) or uninformed ignorance (of the significant documents of recent years). In some circles there is a fear of any implication that anything might actually happen to the bread and wine, which in turn underlies a certain paranoia about the place of the *epiclesis* ('Send the Holy Spirit…') in *Common Worship*.

2. Anti-catholicism includes a deeply-felt **anti-mystical strand**. Despite its own Pietist heritage, much contemporary Evangelicalism is wedded to the Reformation theme of the simplicity and perspicuity of the gospel, compounded and compromised to an almost aggressive degree by the alliance with the secular theme of 'accessibility.' There is a deep-seated suspicion of references to 'mystery' and to anything that is not explicable or 'understanded of the people.'[4]

There is a deep-seated suspicion of references to 'mystery'

3. Furthermore, **Enlightenment rationalism** has influenced Evangelical approaches to the sacrament more than it would care to admit. Unconscious assimilation has gone hand in hand with outspoken rejection, and a 'plain speech' literalist approach to matter reigns. Bread is bread, wine is wine, neither being other than it appears. This routine anti-magic, anti-superstition riposte to any attempts to hint at deeper realities regards the elements of Communion as 'tokens' or 'signs' in a kind of minimalist concession.[5] Evangelicals often unconsciously re-subscribe to the minimizing lens of Zwingli's humanist, memorialist, communitarian theology,[6] increasingly parched by the dessication of time. Functionalist worship, human and worldly, now apes the age which shapes it. So, if 'the abolition of mystery is the essence of Enlightenment,'[7] it is no little irony to find the triumph of the Enlightenment at the heart of Evangelical readings of the sacrament.

4. Such an 'is only' syndrome[8] betrays a thinly veiled **reductionism**, which 'always buys clarity and certitude at the price of mutilating reality.'[9] If the 'mystery…now revealed' (Eph 3.3, 5) is reduced to the solution to a puzzle, and to logical explanations, then explaining *away* has replaced expounding. Such forms of disclaimer-apologies—'Communion is not…; it is simply…'—betray a deep vein of *diminishment*, where the gifts of God in creation and salvation are downgraded, and the sacramental is replaced by the social.[10] The constant suppressed implication of *'Don't take this too seriously!'* meaning 'it's only bread and wine…' reveals a prejudiced, creation-denying reductionism.

The constant suppresse implication of 'Don't take this too seriously!' reveals a prejudiced reductionism

5. In order to disguise this loss of substance, the process of de-mystification is encouraged by a **personalism** which is determined to make everything 'meaningful' and 'real.' Perhaps inevitably, Communion-in-the-round has furthered this process of the horizontalizing of the sacraments which elevates human relationships above the 'vertical.' Ironically, this emphasis on human contact and on community experience has itself been a re-discovery of the charismatic movement, in reaction against the 'dead formalism' of previous generations. However, allied with a loss of a sense of occasion, a patronizing and embarrassing over-familiarity now often displaces any sense of liturgical event or drama, and sets up false patterns of contrived intimacy.

6. This whole process contributes powerfully to **trivializing attitudes**. Holy Communion is now 'the family meal,' representing maybe the final straw in a bourgeoisification of the Lord's Supper, aided and abetted by a paternalistic approach which constantly opts for banality under the guise of simplicity and accessibility. Contemporary Evangelical worship has been far more indelibly shaped by the entertainment industry than it recognizes. Worship, whether supposedly 'all-age worship' or not, has been re-branded into a television game-show. The compère replaces the 'president,' audience replaces congregation, participation becomes pantomime, and *mysterium tremendum* becomes maximum tedium.

Evangelical worship has been far more indelibly shaped by the entertainment industr than it recognizes

7. But perhaps the most commonly-adduced historical grounds for such derogatory attitudes towards the Communion is the **Reformation emphasis on 'the word.'** Word ministries utilize biblical language, especially the Prophets and Paul, to bolster the argument. However, this is often done with little subtlety, and little awareness of the varied significance and contexts of the word 'word' in Scripture. Those Evangelicals who shake their fists at the Procrustean bed of rationalist 'Higher Criticism' need to beware lest the same *tu quoque* argument rebound against them.

It is absolutely correct, for instance, to note the significance of faith in Paul and at the time of the Reformation. But today, so poorly is *sola fide* located theologically that it is in danger of running into the reefs of the blind faith of fideism. In a world where, in parallel to the situation of 250 years ago, deism[11] is the popular religious and 'Christian' response to simplistically-presented scientific discoveries, genuine *theism* again requires hard thinking by Christians in science. Fideism operates most successfully in a deistic world-view, 'blind faith' in the world of the Blind Watchmaker. But the genuine 'experience of faith'[12] only makes sense in a world which is sustained by the priority of *The God who is There* who is love. 'Faith alone,' alone, does not exist without context—even and supremely in Romans. It is dependent on a prior doctrine of God, however much that doctrine is re-forged on the anvil of the Cross.

Similarly, Luther's re-found confidence in the power of the word in the context of late medieval piety is correctly noted, but often incorrectly extended to an isolationism of the word. His belief in the supremacy and uniqueness of the word—*sola fide, solus Christus, sola scriptura*—did not mean that he evacuated the sacrament of its gospel power. For him the word was visible as well as audible. His *sola scriptura* also means quite different things today, when tradition is ignored, from what it did when a fresh theology engaged critically with a long tradition. It is now often little more than a convenient anti-catholic cliché, or a Protestant independence slogan, encouraging autocratic interpretations.

8. For, in those contexts where 'the Word' is the only defining category of Scripture, the Lord's Supper becomes strictly a **non-essential illustrative accessory**, an adjunct, supplementary to the preached word. As in earlier years, Communion is now a theological addendum, something tacked on at the end, after the 'real' ministry—the preaching of the gospel—has taken place. In the world-view where the 'real' necessity is the preaching of the word, Holy Communion can only be an expression of

Communion is now a theological addendum

something made clear elsewhere, and not an embodied demonstration of reconciled lives. But when a fundamental, integral expression of gospel-practice has become an occasional optional extra, then what is being offered as New Testament and Reformation-based doctrine is in fact a body sliced in two: the word without the accompanying sign—half the biblical witness.

Not that most Evangelicals are conscious of this. Evangelical liturgical scholars are of course well aware of the issues, but the ordinary punter is rarely familiar with the history of Anglican or Continental Reformation debates, let alone Catholic or Orthodox viewpoints, and rarely encounters such Christians. This reflects the continuing insularity which has enabled Cranmer to be elevated to a position of virtual papal-Protestant infallibility.[13] Theological and geographical isolationism offer each other mutual support.

9. Ultimately, the fundamental false hidden assumption is that 'real,' 'basic,' 'gospel' **Christianity is non-sacramental**. If the spiritual is the prime, or sole, category, then the material (or confusions of the material and the spiritual, such as are imagined to be the case with non-Protestant doctrines of the Communion) is only secondarily real, and Christianized Platonism has won the day. If the very concept of sacrament itself is 'unbiblical' and 'catholic,' originating as one of the early deformations of church history, the logical corollary is that non-sacramental Protestantism is the true form of the gospel, and that the sacramental traditions of Catholicism and Orthodoxy do not represent 'real Christianity.'[14] Word and sacrament split along the fault-line of Spirit and matter.[15]

Word and sacrament split along the fault-line of Spirit and matter

There is one irony to note before moving on. It is the little-known fact of notable large-scale turnings from Conservative Evangelicalism to the Orthodox Church in the United States in recent years of entire churches and of key leaders of Campus Crusade. Three factors seem relevant:

i) Far from being the un-Reformed and idolatrous[16] church of Evangelicals' fantasies, the Orthodox Church is being read as the *fons et origo* from which the whole Christian church has developed.

ii) The Orthodox Church is seen as generating that perceived depth of spiritual life on which much current Evangelicalism has turned its back.

iii) Its sacramental theology is seen to be rooted in a theology of creation which the Western church, by and large, has lost.

For those former American Evangelicals who have placed Evangelicalism and Orthodoxy in the scales, it is Evangelicalism itself, together with its critique of Orthodoxy, that has been found wanting.

10. We are therefore left with a critical example of the **'falling apart'** of which Tom Torrance repeatedly speaks. Co-inherent realities have been set at war with one another, and a terrible and painful divorce has resulted. Is it at all possible to get behind 'the terrifying arrogance of unshakeable conviction'?[17]

The result is not merely a falling apart, but a tragic offence which pits gospel text against gospel sacrament, and sacramental word against proclaimed word. This yields a double loss—of the word where the sacrament assumes sole importance, and conversely of the sacrament where the word assumes sole importance. By arrogation, each marginalizes the other, producing a split mind in a split church.

Each marginalizes the other, producing a split mind in a split church

Evangelicals who keep polarizing and splitting will keep alienating those drawn towards deep prayer and contemplation, and forfeit the depth they so much need.

3 Second Movement: Forgotten Ground

At the most profound level, such a literally dis-integrating polarization is the child of a deep and largely unconscious Western dualism which prizes thought above action or symbol.

The loss of a vital doctrine of creation demonstrates that split in its most acute form. If Protestantism represents a split within Western Christianity, which itself split from Eastern Christianity in 1054, it is not surprising that Protestantism inherited a particular set of theological problems from its internal genetic history. I shall suggest that the way to a recovery of a properly Evangelical doctrine of Holy Communion can only come by re-integrating the doctrine of creation, which itself involves returning to Scripture and to the witness of the early Christian church.

A critique from the non-Western Evangelical world assists in facing the particular Western dualist split of much contemporary Evangelicalism. In the opening pages of a fine missiological study, Hwa Yung raises the issue of an 'increasing sense of dissatisfaction with a Western theology.'[18] He highlights, firstly, the fact that 'Western theologies are the products of the histories, cultures and realities of the West'; secondly, 'that it presupposes a worldview which has been heavily influenced by the Enlightenment'; thirdly, that 'much of Western theology has been controlled by Enlightenment rationalism and empiricism'; and fourthly, that 'Western theology is often perceived as being built on an idealistic conception of truth which sharply distinguishes it from its practice.'[19] This is not a new critique; but it is a serious non-European summons. Just as Hwa wants Christianity to be properly and scripturally (geographically) contextualized in Asia, so I want to re-contextualize, re-evaluate and re-locate the sacrament (historically and theologically) outside the context of particular medieval debates into a wider scriptural, Evangelical creation base.

'To know' now commonly means 'to be able to prove', to have knowledge of facts

The specific carrier of the deep malaise which underlies these philosophical entrapments is our Cartesian inheritance, where knowledge is frequently (mis-) conceived in idealist[20] terms. 'To know' now commonly means 'to be able to prove,' to have knowledge of facts. *Cogito, ergo sum*; thought demonstrates existence. But a quick glance at the Bible challenges that view instantly, with the conviction that 'to know' means to have an intimate, personal relationship with someone, whether in friendship or marriage or with God. But such a form of 'deep knowing' is often paradoxically denied by the Evangelical tradition itself, caught up in its own forms of idealism, and regarding 'knowledge' as an intellectual, mental decision of faith based on correct, biblical and doctrinal information about God.

Finding Our Proper Place

'Nature' has replaced 'creation'; it is merely stage-scenery, interesting but in the end irrelevant to the text of the play

Within this world-view, the catastrophic suffering of creation is the casualty of 'putting creation in its—wrong, subsidiary—place.'[21] It is seen as strictly secondary, unnecessary, insignificant. 'We'—humanity—are what creation is for; 'it'—creation—matters less. And so matter does not matter. Impersonal 'Nature' has replaced 'creation'; it is merely stage-scenery, interesting but in the end irrelevant to the text of the play. Now, however, we are learning that creation pays the price for our arrogant diminishment of *God's* creation.

The same dangerously functionalist and idealist approach to the sacrament noted above also eliminates creation from theology and practice. Often the only appearance of creation in church contexts is in Alpine calendars or home-made banners. More significant is the fact that turning away from creation constitutes the problem of solipsism:[22] we make ourselves the centre of God's interest instead of the creation of which we are part. The task, rather, is the reverse—to recover a fully biblical doctrine of God's desire for a new heaven and a new earth—transfigured, not eliminated—which will put us in *our* proper place.

It is difficult to place ourselves truly in the position of the early church and the first disciples if we cannot imagine the different world they inhabited. This conceptual gap offers the temptation to construe the early church in our own fantasy image. But, in a way almost impossible to conceive now, the world was then seen as a unitary, material-spiritual single whole, which has been successively taken apart by the split between East and West in 1054, the Reformation-as-internal-theological-debate-in-the-Western-Church from 1517 onwards, the re-Platonized Enlightenment world of ideas and concepts as ultimate reality, the industrial revolution and the technological domination—and ultimately destruction—of creation as something of secondary value. So unless creation is re-introduced into biblical, systematic and eucharistic theology, the sacraments will continue to be downgraded in the Protestant church, and to feature as second-rate ('mere') emblematic tokens of something 'far more real,' that is, faith. It is a modern fallacy to imagine that faith ever flourished without visible signs following, without a total interleaving of the spiritual and the material, without a vast symbolic spiritual superstructure of thought, and without a huge visible rooting in the liturgical traditions of Temple and synagogue.

In the end there is a deep psychic wound in Western Christianity which needs healing. This will come about either by re-examining Scripture without an Enlightenment lens or by rediscovering ourselves as human beings in creation. I am not following Matthew Fox's quest for a 'creation-centred spirituality,' but seeking the significance of the body in a more creation-conscious vision of redemption, Christ being the centre of everything (Colossians 1.17).

This is where the wider Christian world can help poor, talkative Western Christianity

It is a tragedy that Christian mission over recent centuries has exported this European cultural burden around the world so widely. Christianity seems to have been unable to resist the gradually increasing destruction of the world which has taken place not only in those nations which have embraced atheistic Marxism or socialism (such as Russia), but also in those which outwardly are viewed as 'Christian' (such as America). This is where the wider Christian world, perhaps especially Africa, can help poor, talkative Western Christianity. Africans live and die with their bodies, not just their heads.

The ignoring of creation has not only led to the devaluing of the environment; it has also led to a situation in which doctrines of salvation and justification float free from their given Old Testament creational base. In consequence, it has led to doctrines of the sacraments which have become (im-!)purely spiritual and un-earthed. Disconnected from creation, the sacraments have become dematerialized, marginalized and ready for the scrap-heap.

Third Movement: Transfigured Creation[23]

4

Parallel to the deformations of liturgical practice I therefore want to offer a series of reclamations from various periods of history.

Evangelicals' ancestry is broader than they imagine and we need to inhabit a wider landscape than that of Post-Reformation England. Too much Evangelical rhetoric rides on the back of fantasy versions of Catholic-Protestant Hundreds-of-Years War. If the debate only goes back to 1549 (as though 1517 were not more significant), it is inevitably locked into a particular series of definitions and conflicts which prevent a more fundamental biblical and historical vision from emerging. Faithfulness to Evangelical tradition sometimes obstructs faithfulness to Scripture.

Faithfulness to Evangelical tradition sometimes obstructs faithfulness to Scripture

Placing the doctrine of justification by faith in a wider biblical and ontological setting achieves a four-fold gain:

- historically, it releases the debate from being frozen in a juridically-based medieval theology;
- ecclesiastically, it liberates Western Christians from their own form of Babylonian Captivity;
- theologically, it embeds the justice and righteousness of God in the love of the Trinity;
- scripturally, it locates the issue in the context of God's covenantal love with Israel, creation and cosmos (Romans 4.13).[24]

I therefore want to look at four key moments, beginning with Scripture, in order to construct a more biblical vision of the sacrament of Holy Communion.

1. From Israel we learn, firstly, that **creation is fundamental**; Genesis 1 is the starting-point. 'Embodiment is the end of all God's works.'[25] 'Body' means 'earthed'; 'Adam' is linked to the [red] 'ground.' Creation is basic and blessed, even when warped and under judgment. The body is not sinful because it is physical; the mind and the heart are the source of sin ('flesh' in Paul's language).[26] Even though 'flesh' and 'body' can overlap, 'body' is more usually the locus rather than the source of sin.

Judaism has maintained this tradition of the goodness of human and created life much better than the church, which has too often sabotaged the truth by turning the doctrine of original sin (Genesis 3) into a vindictive punishing-machine. Indeed, it is rarely recognized that a Jewish biblical doctrine of creation is foundational to the Christian doctrine of Incarnation, and it is because Evangelicals have too quickly headed for the 'word of the cross'[27] that the pre-requisite doctrines of Christ's human self-emptying and the 'Word become flesh'[28] are underplayed in eucharistic theology.[29]

The basic datum for Communion is therefore correctly bread, and no amount of eucharistic theology should obscure that starting-point. But it is also bread as sign—significant bread, nourishing bread, bread from the earth, the fruit of creation transported and translated to another realm of meaning by being linked with a set of words, a life and a history.

Broken bread signifies real participation in the humanity, brokenness and life of another

Secondly, symbols and signs are an intrinsic element of the gospel and total-biblical witness. The message of Jesus the Word is given in the form not only of words but also of deeds—symbolic deeds and signs. To share bread is to share lives; broken bread signifies real participation in the humanity, brokenness and life of another.[30]

However, Evangelicalism often prefers St Paul's complex doctrinal exposition, and consequently does not take seriously enough either the subtle logic of Jesus' creation-based parables or the healing practice of his speech-acts in the gospels; the intellectually sophisticated Socratic style of his parabolic argument is not noticed. In turn it has rationalized Paul's theology, marginalized his own symbolic world, and ignored references to his powerful charismatic practice.[31]

The parables of Jesus assume that what is true in creation applies to salvation. The argument of many parables depends upon a reliable creation base, for creation is not simply an arena or a stage, but the living object of God's care. Matter means something, has meaning, because it is creation, and because 'the Father' cares for it. 'Not one [sparrow] will fall to the ground apart from your Father' (Matt 10.29). God cares for the birds of the air; therefore (arguing from the smaller to the greater) he will certainly look after you. In reverse, short-lived field-lilies, which do no work, are far more beautiful than Solomon in all his finery. They are the object of God's care!

A right view of matter then changes the meaning of things. In 1 Corinthians, precisely in the context of the social-symbolic significance of eating meals with unbelievers, Paul's discussion of table-fellowship assumes that earthly goods are God's creation.

> Why should my liberty be subject to the judgment of someone else's conscience? If I partake with thankfulness, why should I be denounced because of that for which I give thanks? So, whether you eat or drink, or whatever you do, do everything for the glory of God (1 Corinthians 10.20–31).

Conversely, meanings change the nature of matter. Casual sexual intercourse can easily be understood as fun, natural, pleasure, a laugh, depending on the viewpoint of those involved. 'It didn't mean anything' is a fairly common comment responding to the assumption that it *should* 'mean something.' Committed intercourse within a sexual-social covenant of marriage endows the same act with an entirely different set of meanings and values. This mutuality between matter and meaning is rooted firmly in a doctrine of creator and creation.[32]

The practice of Jesus distinguishes between heaven and earth, but does not divorce dualistically. His miracles ('signs') proclaiming the good news of the reign of God ('the gospel of the kingdom') are predicated upon God's care for the physically broken and God's intention to renew creation. The Sabbath was chosen—and 'broken'—for major healings in order symbolically to redefine it and to demonstrate God's forgiveness and healing in the body.[33] His practice was far removed from modern Western (and even early Eastern) conceptions that the 'soul' is the critical area of God's action and intervention.

His practice was far removed from modern Western conceptions that the 'soul' is the critical area of God's action and intervention

Consequently, we despise creation when we assume that God should always deal with us directly in one particular way. The world is a sacrament, people can communicate (something of) God to us through their faces, touch, smiles, tears, words, pain, which are all part of our sacramental and created interrelatedness not only *for* one another, but *in* one another. One reason for the use of Genesis 1.28 to justify the exploitation of creation is the tragic false anthropocentric assumption of the superiority of humanity over creation. In turn, the heavens no longer seem to declare the glory of God not because God is absent, but because God has been excluded from the visible and expelled into the outer darkness of space.

The notion of sacrament is therefore totally biblical, even though it does not occur in the Bible—not surprisingly, since the word is Latin.[34] Originally used for a soldier's oath, the word soon came to mean (as in Augustine) 'a visible form of an invisible grace.' In it, two only slightly distinguished aspects of reality meet. The first is that, at root, creation can communicate the blessing of God to us; creation can both be and embody blessing. The home of sacraments is creation, where the created is consecrated through prayer to become what early Evangelicals called a 'means' for communicating and receiving the grace of God. Evangelical attacks on the 'pagan' or 'un-biblical' nature of 'sacraments' are therefore totally misplaced, representing an unconscious betrayal of the absence of creation rooting. '"Sacramentalism" attributes meaning and grace to matter.'[35]

The second aspect is that a sacrament is not a substitute for or an alternative to something that happens elsewhere. This parallels the way in which parables are Jesus' preferred form of speech in contrast to our preference for the literal. His words are often literally the secondary response to a prior symbolic action. His interrogatory parables are his riddling retort subsequent to a prior act or sign, not an illustration of something else; they are the message. The parabolic word reinforces the sign and not *vice versa*.[36] Scandalous sign and parable go hand in hand in Jesus' meals with 'sinners' and in his death on the Cross and, in theory, in the celebrating community.

A sacrament is not a substitute for, or an alternative to something that happens elsewhere

There is thus a particularity in the visually articulated practice of the Cross (Eucharist and liturgy) as well as in the verbally articulated preaching of the Cross (*kerygma* and *didache*). A sign is an embedded symbol; a sacrament an embedded sign, an 'effective sign' which bears what it signifies. Christianly speaking, there are no such things as mere symbols. Since we live in a symbolic world, all is symbol; and signs express a specific mysterious ('hidden') reality.[37] They do not point to reality somewhere else. A sign is thus itself the reality proclaimed and a proclamation of God's present reality; Holy Communion is both a sign, bearing reality, and also a sign-bearing reality.

2. The exquisite lyrical and pastoral art of early Christianity and the Trinitarian closeness to creation of Celtic theology highlight their faithfulness to Scripture in this tradition of salvation-in-creation. For early Christian art, creation is both foundational and symbolic; spiritual and ma-

terial intertwine in a way which enabled Christian artists to redesign the cosmos in the image of Jesus Christ and to proclaim the gospel visually to the Graeco-Roman world. The Pauline doctrine of the transformation of the world by the resurrection of Jesus (Romans 8.19–25) is transposed into the key of the artistic and aesthetic Beauty which conquered the world.

The prayer of the Celtic church, in turn, in consonance with the Old Testament, hallowed and sanctified the body and the creation, the ordinary and the everyday. Despite an often fiercely competitive asceticism in history, its modern appeal embraces a desire for the rootedness, rhythm and relationships of the body as part of worship. The phrase 'the offering of *the body* of Jesus Christ once for all' (Hebrews 10.10, my italics) specifically links the physical, historical body of Jesus with the celebration and re-present-ation of that body, surrendered to death, in the bread of the Communion which 'is my body,' and the offering of my own body in response to Christ's—which is absolutely not separated from his, even if its purpose is totally different.[38]

3.   Without entering a doctrinal mine-field, I merely observe that there was no single 'Reformation doctrine' of Holy Communion. There were many, not least those of Luther, Bucer, Calvin, Zwingli and Cranmer. English Evangelicals often speak as if Cranmer was the Reformation, and insist that Cranmerian orthodoxy is the sole basis for Evangelical interpretation of the Communion. But while Cranmer's achievement was immense, it is important to distinguish his doctrines from Luther's and Calvin's, and to enter some cautions exposed over time.

Luther, for example, held much more firmly to a 'realist' view of the sacraments, and certainly to a position of 'consubstantiation,' as opposed to transubstantiation. For him, the traditional prepositional categories (in, with and under) still held, emphasizing the intrinsic link between visible elements and invisible reality. Christ's body and blood are given 'in, with and under' the signs of bread and wine;[39] the created elements and the spiritual gifts co-inhere. The sacrament preached the gospel, the visible word in harmony with the preached word. With no disjunction between hearing and sight, word and sacrament, the biblical text for Luther's theology could be 'Listen! Look!' (Mark 4.3).

For him, Christ's body and blood are given 'in, with and under' the signs of bread and wine

Calvin's[40] understanding of the sacrament was much stronger than often imagined, and he pleaded for a 'frequent use' of Communion: 'no meeting of the church is [to be] held without the word, prayer, the dispensation of the Supper, and alms.' His key language is of representation. Always referring back to Augustine, Calvin uses this word with deliberate ambiguity. The body of Christ is represented symbolically, but it is also re-presented and 'truly exhibited' in two ways: 'by the symbols of bread and wine' (but not in any way identified with them), and supremely 'by the promise' of Christ. The content of Communion is 'Christ with his death and resurrection.'[41]

Cranmer's[42] Communion service is a spiritual-theological exposition of the doctrine of justification by grace through faith. It separates our action (gratitude) absolutely from God's (the sacrifice of Jesus), most significantly by re-locating the first Thanksgiving Prayer from its earlier place in the Prayer of Consecration, and turning (prior) offering into (subsequent) response. The expressive biblical texts inscribed on many Evangelical Holy Tables have been 'Do this in remembrance of me' or 'Till He Come' (1 Corinthians 11.25 and 26), looking respectively to the past or the future.

But all Western Reformation Communion rites can now be seen to lack several crucial elements which have subsequently returned to the church—a truly dynamic trinitarian shaping,[43] a grounded creation base, a vital charismatic sense of the detailed and cosmic ministry of the Holy Spirit in creation and sacrament, a sense of the eloquent inter-penetration of sign and reality, and the deeper meanings of remembrance. On the large canvas, then, the Reformation project of rationalization, simplification and clarification not only deliberately de-coupled many of the excrescences of late medieval worship, but also unconsciously exploded the complex inter-connections of the real symbolic world-view of the Bible and early Christianity, and unwittingly introduced precisely the fixed and formal division between God and creation which it had intended to overcome, and which Deism and science soon proceeded to harden.

4. I turn finally to the period of the **18th and 19th century Evangelicals**, and look at the Communion experience of John Newton, William Cowper and Charles Simeon. I do so because they were all true Evangelical churchmen (Cowper not ordained) who valued the Book of Common Prayer extremely highly. But Cowper and Newton give us seven hymns never published in any Anglican hymnal which illuminate their own high estimation of the sacrament with respect to creation, hearing and sight.

John Newton's Sacramental Hymns, in Book II of his *Olney Hymns*,[44] breathe a deeply devotional spirit, and identify the sacrament in powerful and vivid imagery with the death and presence of Christ. The visual aspect of sacramental proclamation is presented with naïve simplicity, as in Luther's sense of the *verbum visibile*; the word includes the visible.[45] Interestingly, Book II concludes with 21 hymns on 'Creation.'[46]

Firstly, I will look at the first Sacramental Hymn—*Welcome to the table*—which is in fact (as Newton explains in his Preface) a hymn of William Cowper:

This is the feast of heav'nly wine,/ And God invites to sup;
The juices of the living vine/ Were press'd, to fill the cup.

Oh! Bless the Saviour, ye that eat,/ With royal dainties fed;
Not heav'n affords a costlier treat,/ For Jesus is the bread.

The vile, the lost, he calls to them,/ Ye trembling souls, appear!
The righteous in their own esteem/ Have no acceptance here.

Approach, ye poor, nor dare refuse/ The banquet spread for you;
Dear Saviour, this is welcome news,/ Then I may venture too.

If guilt and sin afford a plea,/ And may obtain a place,
Surely the Lord will welcome me,/ And I shall see his face.

Three aspects of Cowper's 'perspicuity, simplicity and ease'[47] leap out—a vital sense of participation in a royal feast, a strong conviction of metaphorical realism, and the vivid sense of sight. Reminiscent of George Herbert's *Love III*, the invitation to a feast is given in the title and opening lines of verses 1, 2 and 4 especially.

The pronounced realist-metaphorical tone, secondly, refuses to pit a bland realism which threatens to overrule the communion elements against 'mere metaphor' which reduces them to illustrative symbolism. Evocatively and suggestively, like Jesus' parables, Cowper uses the language of creation to express the truths of the gospel.

Thus the drink is not simply 'wine' but 'heav'nly wine'; the cup is not simply filled with wine, but with 'the living vine.' The identification between 'Jesus' and 'the bread' is so direct as to indicate the extent of contemporary Evangelicalism's retreat from a potent sense of participation in a feast, and from the realist-metaphorical language which sustains that delight.

John Newton's own hymn *Supplies in the Wilderness*, in a verse not found in the first 1779 edition, speaks of '...his appointed means of grace' in even more daring realist tones:

Jesus, the bread of life, is giv'n/ To be our daily food;
We drink a wondrous stream from heav'n,/ 'Tis, water, wine and
blood.

Thirdly in Cowper's hymn, the vivid sense of the longing of sight forms the climax in the last line: 'And I shall see his face.' This phrase is powerful because unusual, brief and uncomplicated; and subtle because it conveys overtones of key biblical texts which express the present delight and future hope of the believer. It is a measure of the subsequent reaction against this visual emphasis that makes such language now seem so delightfully unfeigned.

Most significantly, however, Cowper is not referring to some future-eschatological expectation, but to an anticipated *present* 'realized-eschatological' reward for the Lord's invitation to 'his Table.' To participate in 'the feast,' in 'the banquet,' to be 'with royal dainties fed,' to drink 'heav'nly wine' here on earth at the Lord's supper, is—here and now—to 'see his face.' To participate in Communion is to see Christ.

The first three verses of Newton's own hymn *Christ Crucified* sustain this vivid sacramental sense. Three times he uses three distinct synonyms to express the aspect of sight ('see,' 'view,' each in alternation, and 'behold'). The element of sight and the engagement of the imagination, so often feared and banned, are given easy hospitality.

In the fourth hymn (*'It is good to be here'*) the language of sight appears most forcefully, not only sensitively nuanced with the language of hearing but clearly linked with emotion. To 'dwell on Golgotha' (verse 1, line 1) involves hearing and seeing in such a way as to effect a patently emotional response to the offer of grace and pardon, as he hears the message and sees the signs of the sin-bearing Lamb of God.

> All my soft affections move, / Weaken'd by the force of love.

The mutuality of tears drawn out in this meditation at Communion, where he weeps in response to the tears of God, is reminiscent of all the centuries of Christian mysticism. He weeps in the presence of the sacrament, which preaches the gospel to him.

> Let me dwell on Golgotha, / Weep and love my life away!
> While I see him on the tree / Weep, and bleed, and die for me!

Writing before the age of fear, then, Newton reminds us of an important and neglected aspect of Evangelical witness and experience.

With Cowper, Newton is one of the major under-rated figures of the beginning of the Evangelical movement of the late eighteenth and early nineteenth century.[48] His emotional and intellectual gratitude for the cross presented in the sacrament, in language indebted to Calvinist, Puritan, Catholic, mystical and Evangelical streams alike, could be a tremendous contribution to today's often effete Evangelical conceptions and non-celebrations of Holy Communion. He also pre-dates the often turgid and costly sacramental debates and controversies of the nineteenth century, which forced many Evangelicals into back-waters and cul-de-sacs of the spirit, in the same way that the discoveries of science forced Christians at large into untenable scriptural and scientific positions. It is time to put those battles behind us and to rediscover the integrity of word and sacrament.[49]

Charles Simeon also deserves mention here, because his own conversion experience took place in the context of an Easter Day Communion service, for which he had felt himself utterly unworthy and unprepared. This is his account, which relates directly to his going up to Cambridge in January 1779:

> I sought to lay my sins upon the sacred head of Jesus; and on the Wednesday began to have a hope of mercy; on the Thursday that hope increased; on the Friday and Saturday it became more strong; and on the Sunday morning (Easter-day, April 4) I awoke early with those words upon my heart and lips, 'Jesus Christ is risen today! Hallelujah! Hallelujah!' From that hour peace flowed in rich abundance into my soul; and at the Lord's table in our chapel I had the sweetest access to God through my blessed Saviour.[50]

Nor was this unique. On a tour in Scotland, we find him 'quite dissolved in tears' at one Communion service, despite repeated frustration with the extremely long sermons; at another, 'Christ was peculiarly precious to my soul.'[51] The high value attached to Holy Communion at this period of Evangelical history was not least due to the context of Simeon's own conversion experience and subsequent influence.[52]

I am not arguing for a naïve return to a rosy past, but for a revisiting of the Evangelical tradition as a way of seeing that it is often larger and more open-ended—within and beyond both Anglicanism and Protestantism—than many realize. I urge that ignoring Evangelical history hinders a fresh and honest reading of certain fundamental aspects of Scripture which are vital, both for the world today, and for the recapturing of a more biblical world-view, which an embattled earlier Evangelicalism was not able to integrate. I have attempted to show, therefore, that the scriptural witness concerning creation, sight, symbol and sign is more important and central than Evangelicals often realize, that the relevant traditions of those outside Evangelicalism are often more biblical than Evangelicals' own, and that Evangelical traditions themselves are often historically, and not scripturally, determined. Without this recognition, people may find that their bed is too short to stretch out on, and the covering too narrow to wrap themselves in (Isaiah 28.10).

5 Coda: 'Enough! The Resurrection'[53]

My final response to the Evangelical criticisms, suspicions and practices in respect of Communion set out in the first part of this paper will be simply to offer a brief series of fresh vistas for thought, bearing in mind that the sacrament of the death of Christ is *both* the heart of the sacrament of creation *and* the heart of the sacrament of the Word.[54] Christ *is*—not merely *was*—the Word made Flesh. Jesus Christ *is* the sacrament of God: the life-giving focus of all our encounter.

a. Despite the formal dependence on Aristotelian logic of the Catholic doctrine of transubstantiation, the issue of the nature, definition and possibility of presence and transformation remains. Far from being self-contradictory nonsense, that doctrine still represents a huge intellectual grappling with the question of what constitutes what is essential and what is accidental to the nature of anything. Simply because we do not always now think in terms of 'substance' and 'accidents' does not mean that the discussion is over. We do not really know what the relationship between mind, body, self and spirit is, and science itself is in a perpetual process of self-reconstitution in the light of ever more baffling phenomena— the contradictions of particle physics, dark matter, anti-gravity and parallel universes. How can such intellectually challenging frontiers of knowledge not also shape our perception of God's quest for us in creation, and our quest in response for an ever-deepening knowledge of the presence of the creator who is also 'The Crucified God'?[55]

How can such intellectually challenging frontiers of knowlege not also shape our perception of God's quest for us in creation

b. It is also easy to imagine that transubstantiation is all that constitutes Catholic sacramental thought. It is not. Karl Rahner's linguistically leaden but philosophically limpid vision of 'transsignification' enables reflection on how contexts change meanings, and *vice versa*. Here, the ordinary and monochrome of our creation and bodies is suddenly 'transsignified' into the full colour of glory when set within the context of the voluntary self-sacrifice of the Son (John 10) for the restoration of the whole creation, as Paul proposes in Romans 8. How can such an event and crucial axis of faith not also raise the deepest questions concerning what, how and where it fills our life with meaning, and where that meaning is most deeply focussed?

c. Eastern Orthodox thought and worship is suffused by a biblical theology of Transfiguration taken from the revelatory moment at the centre of the gospel narratives. As the sun shines and warms the solar system, so the Light of the Word shines on the world (John 1.5, 9) to transform it by its brilliance, and to keep shining, however dark the darkness (John 1). Evangelical Christians who believe that 'prayer changes things' (and people), who claim that God is interested in the smallest details of our lives, who believe that God raised Jesus from the dead, and who believe that the kingdom of this world will become the kingdom of our Lord, and of his Messiah (Rev 11.15), are ideally placed to think, imagine, hope and pray that the very constituent atoms and sub-atomic particles of the universe will be the arena of God's creation, redemption and transfiguration—matter as well as people, to use a false distinction.[56]

d. But also, in a world which so heart-rendingly and criminally perpetuates poverty, how can those emaciated faces, parched skin and empty stomachs not also mirror to us the real poverty of Jesus? In a world which blasphemously wages war on the poor to the tune of billions of dollars every day, does not their cry reach the ears of the Lord of hosts (James 5.4)? And if we celebrate with doctrinal rectitude the death of Jesus, should we not also celebrate it with tears and anguish of mind and heart as we recall that those who oppress or mock the poor insult their Maker (Proverbs 14.31, 17.5)? How do we eat a little fraction of Communion bread while our brother and sister in creation have no daily bread?[57] Here is where we need more of Scripture than is customary to shape both sacramental theology and social commitment.[58]

e. It is offensive and ironic that Protestant dumbing-down of the sacrament has emasculated the liturgy and eliminated any hint of Beauty.[59] Why should we be condemned to worship as though Monteverdi, Tallis and Bach had never written anything 'to the greater glory of God?' What is the blinkered spirit which acts as though Traherne, Blake, Herbert, St John of the Cross or Gerard Manley Hopkins had never written anything, or that the Odes of Solomon and Ephraem's *Hymns on Paradise* had never been penned? It is strange to have dug up the idea that evangelistic endeavours might be assisted by banishing whatever great art the human spirit has birthed. Why have Evangelicals connived with this Great Annihilating Spirit? It is no surprise that the world buys up what the church sells off—Gregorian chant, incense, ritual, silence. One wonders if the world some-times knows better than the church what is of worth, and what in creation is eloquent of its Creator.

f. So much ground-breaking writing and thinking has been done in the area of participation as a theological theme in recent years that it might seem otiose to mention it.[60] But, quite apart from its critical significance for a reading of Isaiah 53, and all consequent theology based on that life-giving passage, it raises the question as to how important it is now to insist in a liturgical context that certain words be said before or after the reception of the Communion elements. This was a question that divided the spirits and burnt enemies at the time of the Reformation. But a fresh per-spective, on the same landscape, on the basis of the same texts, after the storm-clouds have raged, can entirely change the ground of the debate.

As always, truth is at stake in many areas. But this is not a time for retiring into bunkers. It is a time for revisiting Scripture—'whole Scripture,' as Rich-ard Sibbes might have said, in order to construct a more scripturally-based, scientifically cognisant, and theologically visionary conception of the sacra-ment than the tired formulaic clichés often trotted out, in the conviction that all truth is God's truth. Contending for the faith that was once for all en-trusted to the saints requires nothing less than this.

Notes

1   For further discussion on the use of this word, and many other matters touched on rather briefly in this text, please refer to the accompanying Online Resources on the Grove web site at www.grovebooks.co.uk

2   Alan M Stibbs, *The Lord's Supper* (Church Pastoral Aid Society Fellowship Paper Vol XX, No 215, 1958).

3   Note Peter Kuzmic's comment on p 148 of his essay 'History and Eschatology: Evangelical Views,' in Bruce Nicholls (ed), *In Word and Deed* (Exeter: Paternoster, 1995), quoted in John Corrie, 'Creative Tensions in the Mission of the Church: David Bosch Ten Year On,' *Anvil* 18:2 (2001) p 106, n 34: 'Evangelicals seem to find it hard to think in dialectical terms and can hardly endure to live with unresolved questions and amidst tensions.'

4   *The Book of Common Prayer* (BCP), Article XXIV.

5   BCP (Article XXV) specifically states that 'sacraments ordained of Christ be not only badges or tokens of Christian men's profession, but rather they be certain sure witnesses, and effectual signs of grace…'

6   Zwingli's understanding of the Eucharist comprised: 'remembering, giving thanks, coming together, confessing, and pledging'; Ulrich Gäbler, *Huldrych Zwingli: His Life and Work* (Edinburgh: T & T Clark, 1987) pp 131–139, here p 135.

7   Patrick Riley, *Civilizing Sex: On Chastity and the Common Good* (Edinburgh: T & T Clark, 2000) p xvi.

8   Frank Bottomley, *Attitudes to the Body in Western Christendom* (London: Lepus Books, 1979) p 173.

9   Stanley Jaki, *The Road of Science and the Ways to God*. The Gifford Lectures 1974–75 and 1975–76 (Edinburgh: Scottish Academic Press, 1978) p 66 and ch 14: 'The Ravages of Reductionism.'

10   Where an actual liturgy is despised and rejected, another will rush to fill the vacuum. (Note today the customary tea-or-coffee-after-the-service liturgy. Earlier, it was the quasi-sacramental actions of 'coming forward,' 'raising a hand' or 'giving a testimony.') More critically, it betrays a preference for the sacrament of (Christ in?) the neighbour rather than the sacrament of the presence of Christ (in bread and wine).

11   Deism states that, while God may have created the universe, either it has no further need of him, or he has no specific further involvement with it. Many mechanistic Evangelical presentations of the doctrine of God have more in common with such a view of the distance of God from his creation than it would be comfortable to realise. See William Baird, *History of New Testament Research: From Deism to Tübingen* (Minneapolis: Augsburg Fortress, 1992) for the way in which deism birthed modern biblical study.

12   I use here the title of a long and powerful section in Hans Urs von Balthasar, *The Glory of the Lord: A Theological Aesthetics. Volume I: Seeing the Form* (Edinburgh: T & T Clark, 1982) pp 219–425.

13   John Newton warned against this; see the web page accompanying this booklet. (The Evangelicalism of Newton and Simeon).

14 Witness John Stott's seeming disbelief, when his sister is converting to Roman Catholicism, that her priest really believes its sacramental theology 'with all my heart'; Timothy Dudley-Smith, *John Stott: The Making of a Leader* (Leicester: IVP, 1999) pp 333–4.

15 The sacraments do not feature in either the *Alpha* or *Christianity Explored* courses, which seem to have lost contact with any genuinely sacramental form of Christian faith.

16 Idolatry is no preserve of Catholic and Orthodox churches. Richard Sibbes, *The Soul's Conflict with Itself, and Victory over Itself by Faith* [1635], in Alexander B Grosart (ed), *Works of Richard Sibbes*. Volume I (Edinburgh: Banner of Truth Press ([1862–1864], 1973)) p 180, states simply: '[Superstition] transforms God to an idol' in a section where he is treating of the power of the *imagination*.

17 This is a sub-title in the cover article by Don Brewin in the SOMA [Sharing of Ministries Abroad] Newsletter *Sharing*, February 2000, entitled 'Living in opposing worlds—in the same place.'

18 Hwa Yung, *Mangoes or Bananas? The Quest for an Authentic Asian Christian Theology* (Oxford: Regnum Books, 1997).

19 Hwa, *Mangoes or Bananas?*, pp 1–9.

20 I use this word here in its technical philosophical sense, in respect of the supposedly supreme importance of *ideas*, not in reference to *ideals*.

21 Richard Higginson supports this observation, with reference to Australia, in a recent issue of the *Ridley Hall Newsletter* (2001): 'Aboriginal Christianity has a very strong creation spirituality: a sense of God's living, active presence in all created things. In contrast white evangelical Christianity has often had a strong theology of sin and redemption but paid little attention to creation' ('Spirituality Down Under,' p 27).

22 From the Latin *solus ipse*: alone (my)self.

23 See Olivier Clément, *The Roots of Christian Mysticism* (London: New City, 1993).

24 See Tom Wright, *The Letter to the Romans*, in *The New Interpreter's Bible* (Nashville: Abingdon, 2002) Volume X, pp 590–619; note *eg* p 590: 'it is time for a genuinely incarnational theology to be let loose again upon the world.'

25 Chapter heading to Ch X of Jürgen Moltmann, *God in Creation: An Ecological Doctrine of Creation, The Gifford Lectures 1984–1985* (London: SCM, 1985). The German is: 'Leiblichkeit ist das Ende aller Werke Gottes.' See also the interesting Jewish-Christian debate in Tikva Frymer-Kensky *et al*, *Christianity in Jewish Terms* (Boulder, Colorado/ Oxford, UK: Westview Press, 2000) pp 239–268.

26 Bottomley, *Attitudes to the Body*, pp 50–57.

27 For example William J U Philip, *John's Prologue. The Light of Glory*, PT [Proclamation Trust] Media, 2001, pp 10–11. Some Evangelicals are at last rediscovering the Incarnation; see David Petersen (ed), *The Word Became Flesh: Evangelicals and the Incarnation* (Carlisle: Paternoster, 2003).

28 John's use of the word 'flesh' differs here from Paul's. It is used in an Old Testament sense, to refer to the world of fragile, vulnerable, fleeting creation, as in Psalm 103.14f.

29 Ray Simpson of Lindisfarne relates a meeting with a Druid who said, 'I'd be a Vicar if I could believe in the Incarnation.'

30 Walter Brueggemann, *Theology of the Old Testament. Testimony, Dispute, Advocacy* (Minneapolis: Augsburg Fortress, 1997) p 730: 'The Jewish markings of elusiveness, materiality, and concreteness that belong to the very character of Yahweh are what Marcionite Christianity always wants to scuttle. It is the purpose of Christian Old Testament theology, I judge, to pay particular attention to these aspects of Old Testament testimony which are most problematic for Hellenized, Enlightenment Christianity.'

31 See for example Romans 15.18–19, Galatians 3.5.

32 Stanley Jaki, *Creator and Cosmos* (Edinburgh: Scottish Academic Press, 1983).

33 For example Mark 2.28, John 5.9, 17–20, 9.14; Mark 2.1–12 and parallels.

34 The absence of a technical term from the Bible is no proof of its error. Many basic Christian words such as 'trinity,' 'incarnation,' 'Bible' and 'satisfaction,' and phrases such as 'penal substitution' or 'substitutionary atonement' are also not found in the Bible. But note Irving Greenberg's use of the phrase 'the sacramental religion of the Bible' in Frymer-Kensky *et al*, *Christianity in Jewish Terms*, p 152.

35 Bottomley, *Attitudes to the Body*, p 172.

36 Kenneth E Bailey, *Poet and Peasant and Through Peasant Eyes: A Literary-Cultural Approach to the Parables in Luke* (Grand Rapids: Eerdmans, 1983) pp 1–43, esp pp 17–18; and *Finding the Lost: Cultural Keys to Luke 15* (St Louis: Concordia, 1992) pp 15–53, esp pp 15–22.

37 *cf* Riley, *Civilizing Sex*, pp 92–93: 'Now that thinkers of our time have investigated the manifold functions of symbol, they are better able than those of the nineteenth century to find their way out of the desert of solipsistic logic that Descartes created when he destroyed the validity of sense perception and with it the utility of symbol.'

38 Frances Ridley Havergal's 1874 'Take my life…' (hands, feet, voice, lips, silver, gold, intellect, will, heart, love, myself) seems to be an equally and detailedly earthed variant of the 1558 Sarum Primer's 'God be in my head…' (understanding, eyes, looking, mouth, speaking, heart, thinking, end, departing).

39 See the full text of the chorale-hymn 'Deck thyself, my soul, with gladness' on the web page accompanying this booklet.

40 See Brian A Gerrish, *Grace and Gratitude. The Eucharistic Theology of John Calvin* (Edinburgh: T & T Clark, 1993).

41 Calvin, *Institutes of the Christian Religion*, IV, 17, 44 (frequency), 11 ('exhibited' and content). See www.ccel.org.c/calvin/institutes. *cf* François Wendel, *Calvin: The Origin and Development of His Thought* (London: Collins Fontana, 1965) pp 329–355.

42 See Peter N Brooks, *Thomas Cranmer's Doctrine of the Eucharist: An Essay in Historical Development* (Basingstoke: Macmillan, 1992).

43 See Bishop Hilarion Alfeyev, *The Mystery of Faith. An Introduction to the Teaching and Spirituality of the Orthodox Church* (London: DLT, 2002) p 139: 'The eucharistic celebration is Trinitarian in nature.'

44 The accompanying resources web page has a full text of these hymns and other material; see also James M Gordon, *Evangelical Spirituality: From the Wesleys to John Stott* (London: SPCK, 1991) on Newton and Cowper, pp 67–92.

45 The Revd Kristin Ofstad and Bishop Graham Dow have both given powerful accounts of the effect of outdoor celebrations of the Eucharist in Oslo and in Coventry.

46 The titles of these hymns can be found on the accompanying web page.

47 These are the terms of Newton's characterisation of his own hymns in the *Preface*.

48 Kenneth Hylson-Smith, in *Evangelicals in the Church of England: 1734–1984* (Edinburgh: T & T Clark, 1984) pp 37–40 (here p 37), describes Newton generously, but not without some exaggeration, as 'not only one of the most remarkable of the Evangelical leaders, but arguably one of the most remarkable men in the whole history of the Church of England.'

49 Some brief earlier reflections on this theme of the integrity of Word and Sacrament appeared in Ian Bunting (ed), *Celebrating the Anglican Way* (London: Hodder & Stoughton, 1996) pp 97–102.

50   William Carus (ed), *Memoirs of the Life of the Rev'd Charles Simeon, with a Selection from his Writings and Correspondence* (London: Hatchard, 1847) p 9. In terms of synchronization, it is worth recollecting that John Newton dates the Preface to the first edition of his *Olney Hymns* to 15th February, 1779, half-way between Simeon's matriculation and his first Communion following his period of anguished preparation.

51   Carus, *Memoirs*, p 120 (19 June, 1796) and p 125 (10 July, 1796).

52   See G C B Davies, 'Simeon in the Setting of the Evangelical revival,' and Arthur Pollard, 'The Influence and Significance of Simeon's Work,' in Arthur Pollard and Michael Hennell (eds), *Charles Simeon: 1759–1836. Great Anglicans* (London: SPCK, 1964) pp 9–26 and 159–184. See also Hugh Evan Hopkins, *Charles Simeon of Cambridge* (London: Hodder & Stoughton, 1977).

53   Gerard Manley Hopkins, 'That Nature is a Heraclitean Fire and of the comfort of the Resurrection.'

54   See Donald Coggan, *The Sacrament of the Word* (HarperCollins/STL, 1987). The American title is more narrowly re-located as *Preaching: The Sacrament of the Word* (Crossroad 1988)—but Calvin would have approved. See Gerrish, *Grace and Gratitude*, ch 3: 'The New Heir and the Sacramental Word,' esp pp 82–86.

55   See most recently Richard Bauckham, *God Crucified* (Carlisle: Paternoster, 1998).

56   See, magnificently, Olivier Clément, *The Roots of Christian Mysticism*, pp 95–129 ('Ecclesia: A Place for Rebirth') here p 110: 'By his death and resurrection [Christ] has brought glory to the universe. It is this transfigured creation that is offered to us in the Eucharist'; and pp 166–177 ('Passions Transfigured, Thought Transcended') here p 176: 'Nothing exists—anger or lust—that does not have some share in what is good. That fact is the basis of metamorphosis.'

57   Liberation Theology is easy for Western Christians to snipe at—until they confront poverty. Tissa Balasuriya, *The Eucharist and Human Liberation* (London: SCM, 1977), raised this question long ago.

58   It is not difficult here to recall the vigorous writings of Kenneth Leech, such as *True God: An Exploration in Spiritual Theology* (London: SPCK, 1985).

59   See Paul Evdokimov, *The Art of the Icon: A Theology of Beauty* (Oakwood Publications, 1991).

60   See John Zizioulas, *Being as Communion* (London: DLT, 1985); Alan J Torrance, *Persons in Communion: An Essay on Trinitarian Description and Human Participation* (Edinburgh: T & T Clark, 1996); Paul Fiddes, *Participating in God: A Pastoral Doctrine of the Trinity* (London: DLT, 2000); and Nicholas Sagovsky, *Ecumenism: Christian Origins and the Practice of Communion* (Cambridge: CUP, 2000).